Alfred's max

Keyboard 1

see it ◉ hear it ◉ play it

AMY ROSSER
NATHANIEL GUNOD

Alfred's MAX™ is the next best thing to having your own private teacher. No confusion, no frustration, no guesswork—just lessons that are well paced and easy to follow. You listen to the music you're learning to play and watch a professional show how it's done, then get time to stretch out and put it all together. No matter how you like to learn, Alfred's MAX™ series gives you the ultimate learning experience at a screamin' deal of a price.

D1607031

Cover foreground keyboard photo by Karen Miller.
Cover background keyboard photo courtesy of Yamaha Corporation of America.

Alfred
ap

CONTENTS

About the DVD

The DVD contains valuable demonstrations of all the instructional material in the book. You will get the best results by following along with your book as you watch these video segments. Musical examples that are not performed with video are included as audio tracks on the DVD for listening and playing along.

HOW TO USE THIS BOOK AND DVD

Alfred's MAX™ Keyboard 1 provides all the information you need to get started playing any keyboard instrument. The book and DVD may be used together or separately. The DVD contains video demonstrations of the pieces and exercises in the book plus further explanations of techniques and musical concepts to further help you reach your maximum potential on the keyboard.

Like most students, you may find it best to have your DVD player positioned near your instrument so that you can use the book as you watch and play along with the video. Sometimes you might prefer to work first with the book before using the video, carefully reading the instructions and playing the music. Other times, you may want to start by watching the demonstration. You decide what works best for you. There is no wrong way to use an Alfred's MAX book and DVD!

If you have an acoustic piano, whether it is a spinet, upright, or grand piano, you have all of the advantages of wonderful *touch sensitivity*. This means that you will be in complete control of the type of piano sound you make.

If you are just getting started and do not own a piano, it is a good idea to buy an electronic keyboard that is completely portable. Many keyboards will even operate with batteries and have their own internal speakers. Perhaps the most interesting feature of an electronic keyboard is the opportunity to choose different sounds for each piece of music. You will find suggestions in this method for different sounds to use. When shopping for an electronic keyboard, it is a good idea to choose one that has touch-sensitive keys so that you can vary the loudness and softness of the music with the force of your touch.

Here are some important things anyone learning to play music should keep in mind:

- **It is better to practice a little a lot than to practice a lot a little.** In other words, never miss a day of practice, even if you spend just a few minutes. Skipping a few days of practice and then practicing once for a long time will not be nearly as helpful as regular practice.

- **The quickest way to play fast fluently is to take the slowest route.** You will learn to play fast music by practicing slowly. Playing too fast too soon can lead to confusion, difficulty and bad habits that will slow your progress. The tortoise wins the race!

- **Practice with a metronome.** A metronome is an adjustable device that beats time for you. Electronic metronomes are inexpensive and very accurate. Get one that makes a click loud enough for you to hear. Practicing with a metronome will teach you to play with correct rhythm.

Although this book is perfect for a self-directed student, **there is no substitute for a good teacher.** A teacher can watch and listen to you play, and give you guidance and encouragement to do your best.

SITTING AT YOUR INSTRUMENT

Sitting at the Piano

- The bench must face the keyboard squarely.
- Sit on the edge of the bench exactly in front of the middle of the keyboard.
- Lean slightly forward.
- Relax and let your arms hang loosely from the shoulders.
- Adjust the distance of the bench from the keyboard so that when your hands are on the keyboard, your arms are parallel to the floor.
- Your knees should be slightly under the keyboard.
- Your feet should be flat on the floor. One foot may be slightly forward.

Sitting at the Electronic Keyboard

This is exactly the same as sitting at the piano, but be careful with the height of the stand or table on which the keyboard is sitting. Adjust the keyboard stand or the table/chair combination you are using so that your arms are perpendicular to and level with the keyboard.

HAND AND FINGER POSITION

- Curve your fingers. From above, you should see a row of knuckles but no fingernails.

- Curve the thumb slightly inward. No hitchhiker thumbs!

- There should be a hollow spot big enough for a ping-pong ball to fit in your palm.

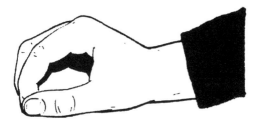

- Fingers are used like levers with the motion coming from the joint that attaches the finger to the hand.

- Push the keys down with the tips of the fingers.

- Keep your fingernails very short!

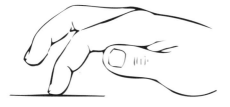

Fingering

Fingering numbers, which appear as the numbers 1 through 5, show which fingers to use to play. They can be found above or below the music. Each number corresponds to the same finger on either hand, with both thumbs being number 1 and both pinkies being number 5.

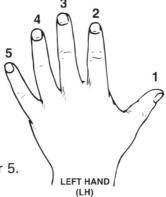

LEFT HAND (LH)

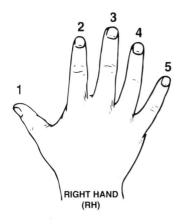

RIGHT HAND (RH)

THE KEYBOARD AND PITCH

The *keyboard* is made up of white and black *keys*. These keys are laid out in a repeating pattern, with black keys in groups of two and three. Each group of black keys is separated by two white keys.

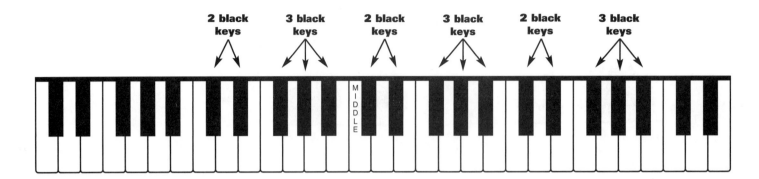

2 black keys **3 black keys** **2 black keys** **3 black keys** **2 black keys** **3 black keys**

Pitch is the highness or lowness of a sound. On the piano keyboard, the pitch goes down to the left, and goes up to the right. As you move to the left, the pitches sound lower. As you move to the right, the pitches sound higher.

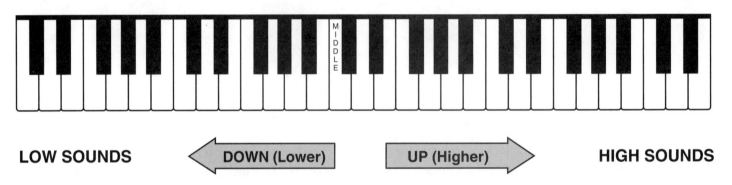

LOW SOUNDS ← DOWN (Lower)   UP (Higher) → **HIGH SOUNDS**

Award-winning pianist and singer/songwriter Norah Jones brought new attention to jazz keyboard sounds with her 2002 album *Come Away With Me.* Her unique blend of pop and jazz has made her one of the world's most popular performers.

FINGER WARM-UPS ON THE BLACK KEYS

To get your fingers moving on the keyboard, play these exercises on the black keys.
The illustrations show which fingers to use on which black keys.

The numbers represent the fingers you will use to play.
Read from left to right and play at a slow, even pace.

Black-Key Warm-up for the Right Hand

RH

1	2	3	2	1	1	1
1	2	3	2	3	4	4
5	4	3	2	1	1	1
1	2	3	4	5	1	1

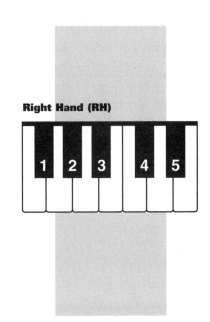

Right Hand (RH)

Black-Key Warm-up for the Left Hand

LH

5	4	3	4	5	5	5
5	4	3	4	3	2	2
1	2	3	4	5	5	5
5	4	3	2	1	5	5

Left Hand (LH)

writing.

THE MUSICAL ALPHABET AND THE NAMES OF THE WHITE KEYS

There are seven letters in the *musical alphabet:*

A B C D E F G

They repeat over and over:

A B C D E F G A B C D E F G A B C and so on.

Every key on the piano has a name from the musical alphabet. The illustration below shows the names of the white keys. Notice that the C nearest the middle of the keyboard is called *middle C.* This is an important marker to memorize.

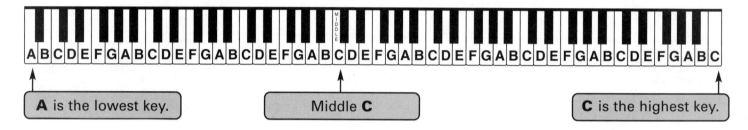

A is the lowest key. Middle **C** **C** is the highest key.

If you are using an electronic keyboard with fewer than 88 keys, middle C is still the C closest to the middle of the keyboard. The highest and lowest notes, however, may be different than those shown above.

Notice that every C is always directly to the left of a group of two black keys.

Every F is directly to the left of a group of three black keys.

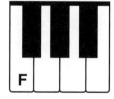

Find all of the C's and all of the F's on your keyboard.

FINGER WARM-UPS ON THE WHITE KEYS

Now let's try playing on the white keys. In these warm-ups, the notes are black circles with the name of the key to be played inside. The finger numbers appear **above** notes played with the right hand (**RH**) and **below** notes played with the left hand (**LH**).

One of the reasons that music notation is easy to read is that it looks the way it sounds. As the pitch goes up, the notes look higher on the page; as the pitch goes down, the notes look lower on the page. The warm-ups below are great examples of this.

Right-Hand Warm-up No. 1

Start on middle C. This is the right-hand C Position.

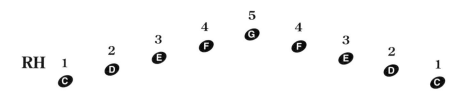

Right-Hand Warm-up No. 2

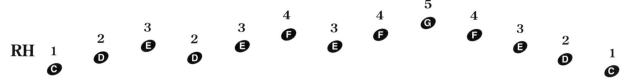

Left-Hand Warm-up No. 1

Start on the C below middle C. This is the left-hand C Position.

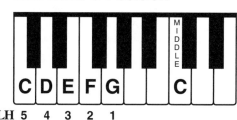

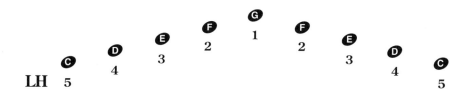

Left-Hand Warm-up No. 2

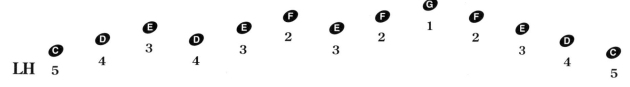

RHYTHM

Rhythm is the arrangement of long and short sounds into patterns. We measure the lengths of these sounds by counting *beats*. A beat is a unit of musical time; it is the pulse that keeps the music alive. When you tap your foot as you listen to music, you are tapping the beats.

We write rhythms with notes.

Play four quarter notes on middle C with your right hand. Count four steady beats aloud ("1, 2, 3, 4"), giving each quarter note one beat.

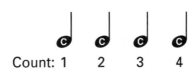

Count: 1   2   3   4

Play two half notes on middle C with your right hand.
Count four steady beats aloud, giving each half note two beats.

Count: 1   2   3   4

Play a whole note on middle C with your right hand.
Count four steady beats aloud.

Count: 1   2   3   4

Using the music below as a guide, first play four quarter notes on middle C with your right hand, one note for each count. Then, play two half notes, playing one note for every two counts. Then play a whole note, counting to four while you hold the note. Each group of four counts, or beats, is called a *measure*. Music is divided into measures with *bar lines*, and a *double bar* is used at the end.

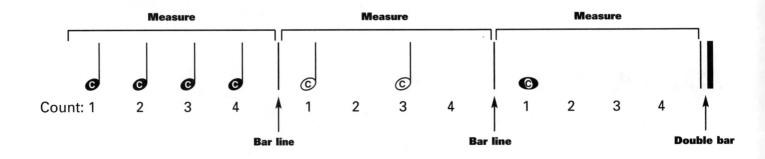

Enjoy playing these melodies. At first, count aloud as you play.

After you learn to play these, experiment with your electronic keyboard and try playing them with some interesting sounds.

Merrily We Roll Along

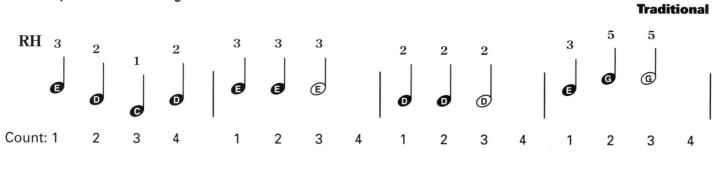

Go Tell Aunt Rhody

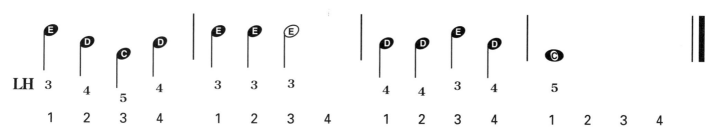

Aura Lee

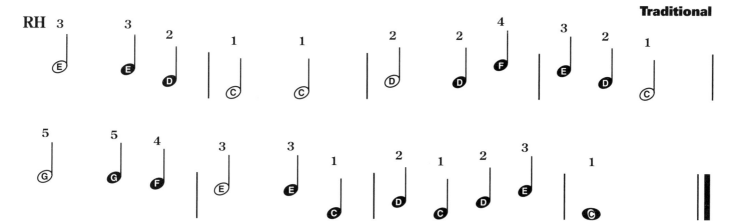

TIME SIGNATURES

At the beginning of every piece of music are numbers called the *time signature*. The time signature tells us how to count the music.

The top number tells how many beats are in each measure. A **4** means there are **four** beats in each measure.

The bottom number tells what kind of note gets one beat. A **4** means a **quarter note** ♩ gets one beat.

Right in Time

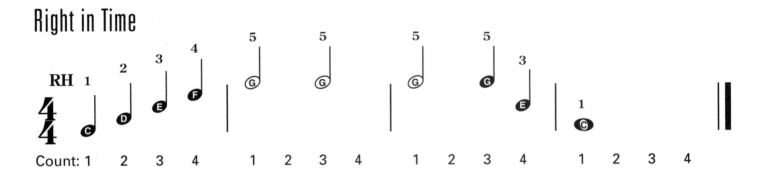

Count: 1 2 3 4   1 2 3 4   1 2 3 4   1 2 3 4

Four Beats Left to Go

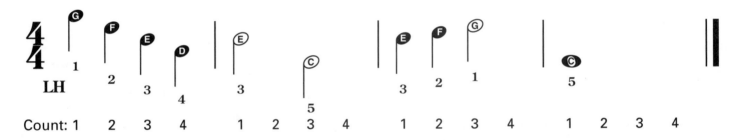

Count: 1 2 3 4   1 2 3 4   1 2 3 4   1 2 3 4

Billy Joel discovered classical piano music at the age of four, and his love for the style that provided such a great technical foundation for his playing has never ended. With a smart urban sensibility and tremendous talent for composing music in a variety of styles, he is considered to be one of the most influential singer/songwriters of our time.

Photo: © Ken Settle

Count carefully and keep a steady beat.

Try a flute sound for these pretty tunes!

Time for Both

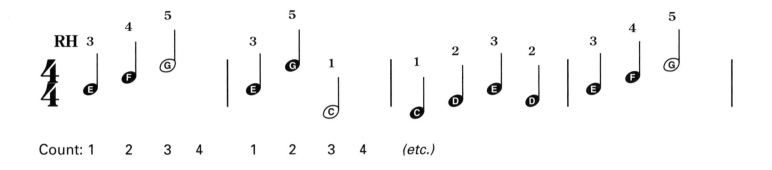

Count: 1   2   3   4   1   2   3   4   (etc.)

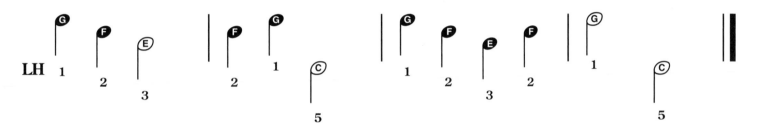

Au Clair de la Lune

French Folk Song

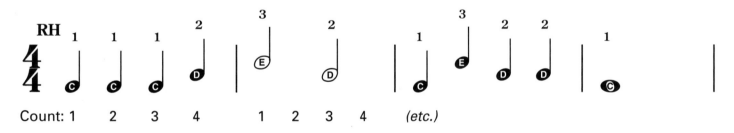

Count: 1   2   3   4   1   2   3   4   (etc.)

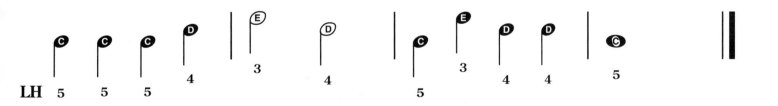

THE TREBLE STAFF

In music notation, specific notes are indicated by their placement on a *staff*, which is made of five horizontal lines and the four spaces in between.

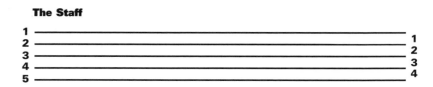

Music for the right hand is written on the *treble staff*, which is marked with a *treble clef*. The treble clef is sometimes called the *G clef* because the line it encircles is called G. A note placed on that line will be a G note.

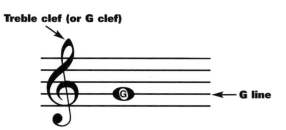

As the music moves up through the musical alphabet, each note is written on the next-higher space or line. As the music moves down—backward through the alphabet—each note is written on the next-lower space or line. Notice that D is written on the space just below the staff, and middle C is written on a short line below the staff called a *leger line*.

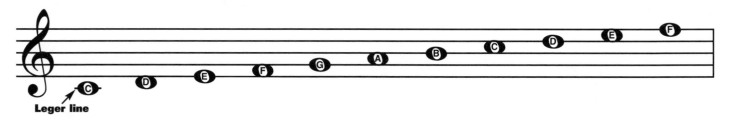

The spaces of the treble staff are easy to remember because, from bottom to top, they spell the word **FACE**.

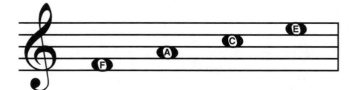

You can remember the notes on the lines of the treble staff using the sentence **E**very **G**ood **B**oy **D**oes **F**ine.

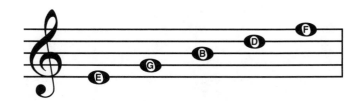

Here is the right-hand C position and the notes on the treble staff.

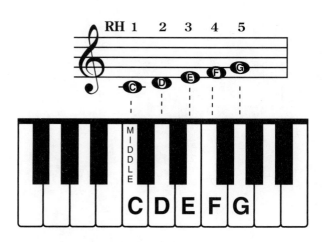

Here are some C-position pieces on the treble staff for you to play. As you can see, the music still looks the way it sounds: As the pitch ascends, the notes look higher on the page; as the pitch descends, the notes look lower on the page. Longer notes take more space, shorter notes take less space.

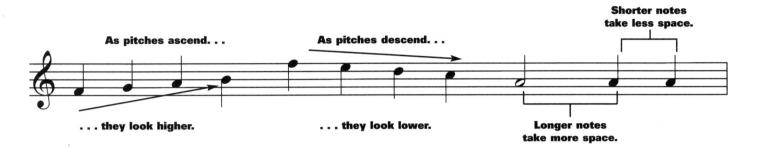

Old Woman on the Right

Traditional

Mary Had a Little Lamb

Traditional

THE BASS STAFF

Music for the left hand is written on the *bass staff,* which is marked with a *bass clef.* The bass clef is sometimes called the *F clef* because the line surrounded by the dots is called F. A note placed on that line will be an F note.

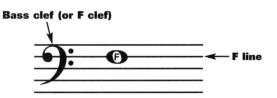

Just like the notes on the treble staff, as the music moves up through the musical alphabet, each note is written on the next-higher space or line. As the music moves down, each note is written on the next-lower space or line.

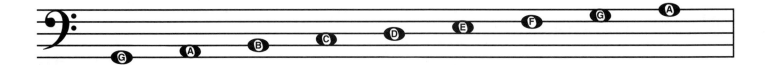

You can remember the notes on the spaces of the bass staff using the sentence **A**ll **C**ows **E**at **G**rass.

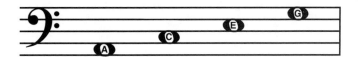

You can remember the notes on the lines of the bass staff using the sentence **G**reat **B**ig **D**ogs **F**ight **A**nimals.

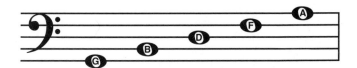

Here is the left-hand C position and the notes on the bass staff.

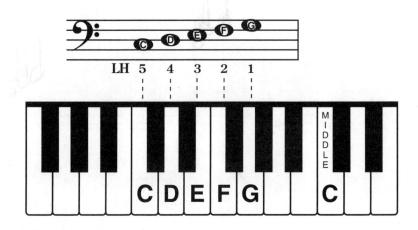

Here are some C-position pieces on the bass staff for you to play.

> *Have fun finding some sounds that work for low notes, such as a bass guitar or tuba sound.*

Old Woman on the Left

Traditional

Frère Jacques

French Folk Song

During a time when the guitar dominated the world of music, Elton John redefined the role of the piano in rock. With a flamboyant style of performing, he became one of the most influential keyboard artists of the 1970s and 1980s. In addition to a phenomenal recording career, he has achieved great success as a composer for hit Broadway musicals such as *Aida* and the *Lion King*.

Photo: © Ken Settle

THE GRAND STAFF

Piano music is written on a *grand staff*, which has a treble staff
and a bass staff that are connected by barlines and a *brace*.

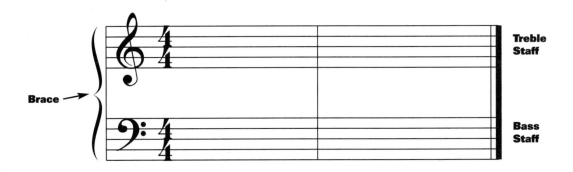

Here is C position and the notes on the grand staff.

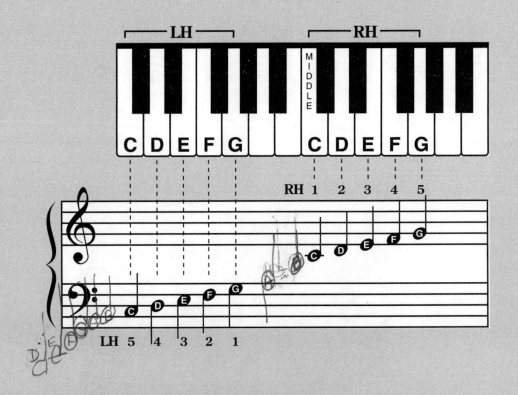

THE WHOLE REST

A *whole rest* indicates an entire measure of silence.

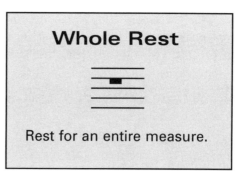

Whole Rest

Rest for an entire measure.

The following pieces will give you some practice reading music on the grand staff. Notice that while one hand is playing, the other is resting.

Try a big orchestral sound for this melody from Beethoven's Ninth Symphony.

Ode to Joy

Ludwig van Beethoven

Count: 1 2 3 4   (etc.)

Frère Jacques—Right and Left

French Folk Song

Below is another version of "Ode to Joy." This time, you'll play with both hands together. Keep your hands in C position and keep your eyes on the music. Learning to play by "feel" will make you a better sight-reader.

Practice Tip: It is helpful to learn each hand individually before playing with both together.

Ode to Joy (with Two Hands)

Ludwig van Beethoven

Merrily We Roll Along

Traditional

THE HALF REST

A *half rest* indicates two beats of silence.

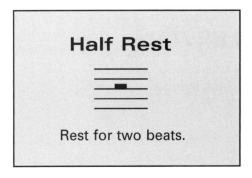

Be careful not to confuse the half rest with the whole rest. Notice that the half rest sits on top of the third line while the whole rest hangs below the fourth line.

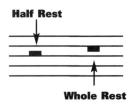

This exercise will prepare you for "Lightly Row," which combines half rests in one hand with notes in the other.

Lightly Row

Traditional

THE QUARTER REST

A *quarter rest* indicates one beat of silence.
It looks a little bit like a bird flying sideways.

Quarter Rest

Rest for one beat.

The following pieces will let you concentrate on counting rests because they use only one hand at a time.

Quarter March

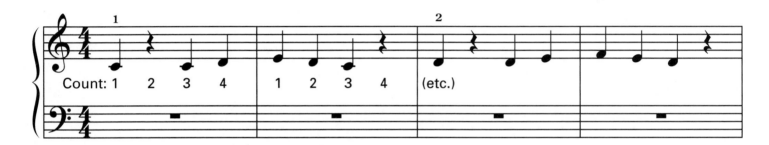

Count: 1   2   3   4   1   2   3   4   (etc.)

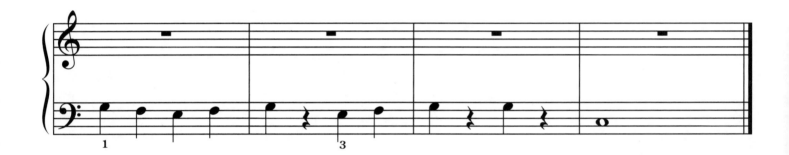

A Restful Day

Count: 1   2   3   4   1   2   3   4   1   2   3   4   1   2   3   4

(etc.)

Let's put the hands back together. First, learn each hand individually, counting carefully. Remember to keep your eyes on the music.

A Stitch in Time

Anna's March

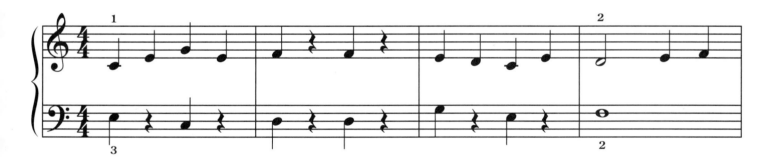

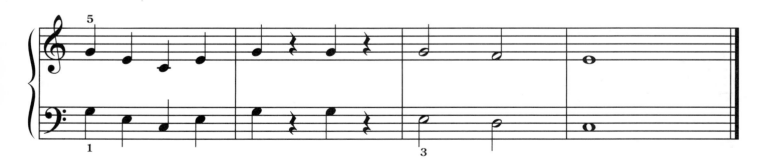

DYNAMIC MARKINGS

One of the ways we make music more enjoyable and interesting is by varying the volume at which we play. Musicians refer to these changes in volume as *dynamics*, and *dynamic markings* are used in written music to indicate the various degrees of loud and soft.

Below are two important dynamic markings. Each one is an abbreviation of an Italian word that describes the volume. (Italian is the international language of music.)

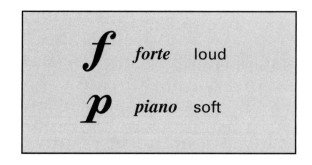

On a keyboard with weighted keys (such as an acoustic piano and some electronic keyboards), play loud by using more weight in the arm and wrist as you drop into the key; use less weight to play soft. On a keyboard that does not have weighted keys, use a more forceful finger motion to play loud, and use a more gentle finger motion to play soft.

Electronic Keyboards: If you are playing an electronic keyboard with touch-sensitive keys, you will be able to affect dynamics with your fingers as described above. If your keyboard does not have touch-sensitive keys, you may have to change the sound selection or use the volume control to create changes in dynamics.

Play all the loud notes equally loud and all the soft notes equally soft.
Keep a steady beat, and be careful not to play faster when you play louder or slower when you play softer. Have fun with this study in contrasts.

Loud and Soft

Here is another important dynamic marking:

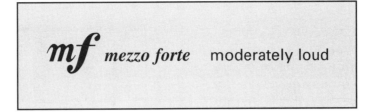

Concentrate on making a clear difference between the different dynamics in this piece.

Three Ways to Play

Tori Amos began playing piano at the young age of two and a half. With her original, technically fluid keyboard stylings and remarkable talent for elegant, inventive songwriting, she began attracting what is now a huge loyal following with the release of her 1992 album *Little Earthquakes*.

Photo: © Ken Settle

MELODIC 2NDS

An *interval* is the distance between two notes. On the keyboard, the interval from one white key to another adjacent white key, up or down, is called a *2nd*. When two notes are played one after the other, as notes are played in a melody, the interval is called a *melodic interval*.

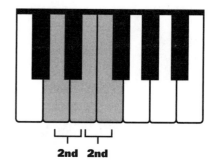

Notice that 2nds are written from a **line to a space**, or a **space to a line**.

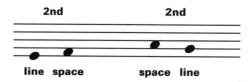

Some of the melodic 2nds in the following piece are labeled for you; see if you can label the rest.

Who's on Second?

MELODIC 3RDS

To play a 3rd, skip a white key.

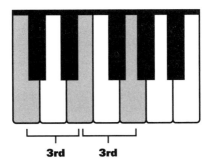

Notice that 3rds are written from a **line to a line**, or a **space to a space**.

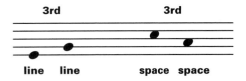

Some of the melodic 3rds in the next piece are labeled. Try labeling the rest yourself.

Third Dimension

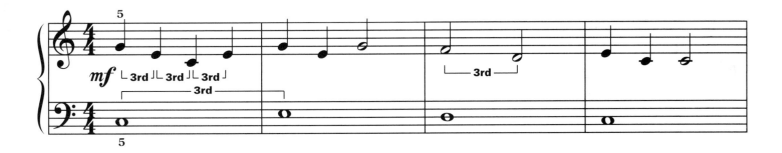

HARMONIC 2NDS & 3RDS

When we play two notes together, we create *harmony*, and the intervals between these notes are called *harmonic intervals*. The 2nds and 3rds you have learned as melodic intervals can also be played as harmonic intervals.

Play these harmonic 2nds and 3rds, and notice that the 2nds have a *dissonant* (clashing) sound and the 3rds have a *consonant* (harmonious, sweet) sound.

Now that you're playing notes together with a single hand, it is even more important to learn each hand separately before putting them together.

Sweet and Sour

MELODIC 4THS

To play a 4th, skip two white keys.

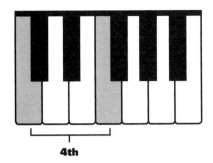

4th

Notice that 4ths are written from **line to space** or **space to line**, like 2nds. You will find that this is true for all even-numbered intervals.

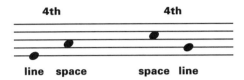

4th   4th

line   space   space   line

Some of the 4ths in this piece are labeled; you label the rest.

Go Fourth and Make Music!

MELODIC 5THS

To play a 5th, skip three white keys.

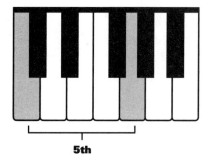

5th

Notice that 5ths are written **line to line** or **space to space**, like 3rds. You will find that this is true for all odd-numbered intervals.

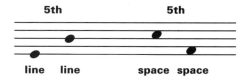

5th   5th

line   line   space space

Fifth Avenue   One 5th is labeled in the following piece; you label the rest.

After more than four decades, jazz and fusion great Chick Corea continues to enjoy a career that reflects the evolution of contemporary keyboard playing. With such diverse influences as Mozart, Charlie Parker, Beethoven and Bud Powell, his innovations include exciting experimentation with electronic music.

Here's a tune that's played in middle C position. Say the names of the notes aloud as you play until the bass clef A and B notes are fully learned.

Middle C Rock

Whether it's blues, rock, country, or gospel, Ray Charles has mastered them all. His versatility and command of the keyboard have made this legendary singer, songwriter and composer one of the most popular entertainers of all time.

THE FLAT SIGN

A *flat sign* ♭ before a note means to play the next key to the left, whether it is a black key or a white key.

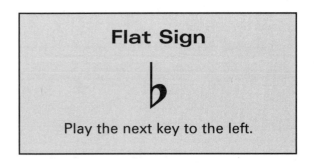

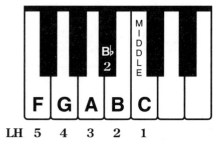

A flat sign is one of several symbols that are called *accidentals*. When an accidental appears before a note, it applies to that note for the rest of the measure. If the accidental does not appear again in the next measure, the note in question returns to its natural position.

This tune is played in middle C position and includes some flat notes.

Try an organ sound for this bluesy tune.

B Flat, B Blue

These pieces will give you some more practice reading flats in middle C position.

Walk in the Park

Rockin' All Night Long

G POSITION

G position introduces several new notes: low B, low A, and low G in bass clef
for the left hand and A, B, high C, and high D in treble clef for the right hand.

Here is G position and the notes on the grand staff.

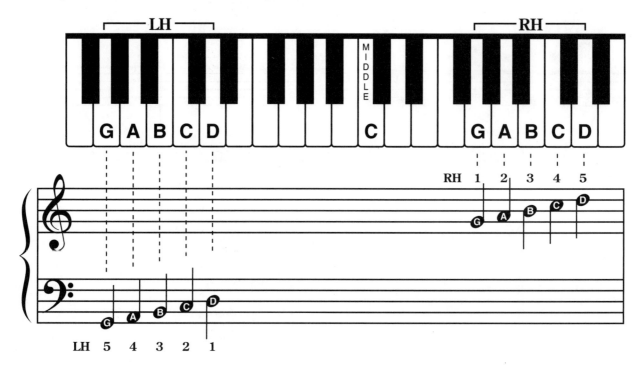

Practice playing the notes in G position, reciting the names of the notes aloud as you play.

HARMONIC 3RDS, 4THS AND 5THS

This exercise will prepare your left hand to play the next piece. It uses harmonic 3rds, 4ths and 5ths.

Be sure to learn each hand alone before playing hands together. Practice slowly at first.

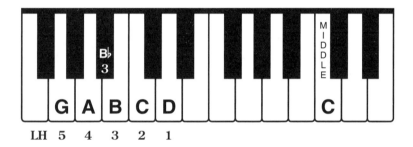

This piece has a definite rock 'n' roll feel, so try one of your keyboard's cool synth sounds. It will also sound great with an electric piano sound.

G Rock

TIED NOTES

A *tie* is a curved line that connects two notes of the same pitch. Two notes connected by a tie are *tied notes*. The second tied note is not struck; rather, the key is held down for the combined values of both notes.

This is a great way to write notes that are longer than one measure...

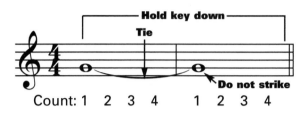

...or to start a long note on the fourth beat of a measure.

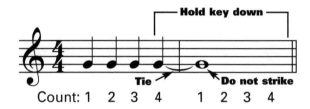

In this C-position exercise, the right hand has notes tied over the bar line into measures 2, 4 and 6. Meanwhile, the left hand plays on the first beat of every measure. Count aloud as you play.

Tie Exercise

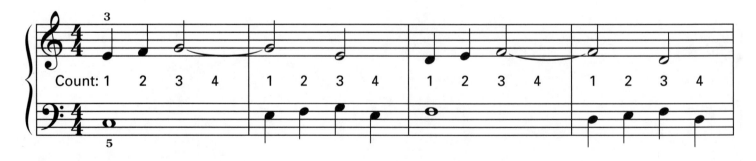

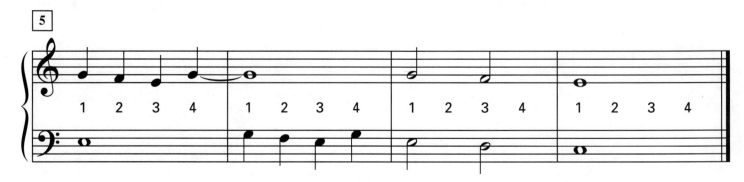

DOTTED HALF NOTES

Adding a dot to the right of a note increases its value by half. Since a half note gets two beats, a dotted half note gets three. A dotted half note is equal to a half note tied to a quarter note.

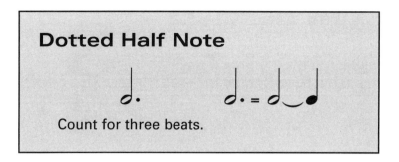

Dotted Half Note

Count for three beats.

Next New Year's Eve, you can entertain your fellow revelers with this classic tune, which is almost all in C position. In measure 7, reach with your second finger to play E and your hand will be perfectly positioned for your fifth finger to play the A in measure 8 without having to reach. Also, notice that the melody starts in the left hand and moves to the right, then returns to the left hand at the end.

> *Choose a great holiday sound that will be heard over the merriment, such as brass or string orchestra.*

Auld Lang Syne

Traditional Scottish Melody

¾ TIME SIGNATURE

Often called *waltz time*, ¾ time has three beats per measure.

3 A **3** means there are **three** beats in each measure.

4 A **4** means a **quarter note** ♩ gets one beat.

Anna's Waltz

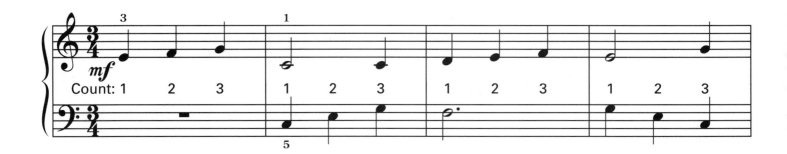

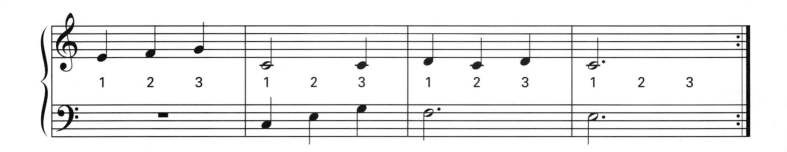

Sarah McLachlan studied classical guitar, piano and voice before signing her first recording contract at the age of 17, and has since become a three-time Grammy Award winner. In 1997, she founded the Lilith Fair, a music tour that focused on female singer/songwriters.

Photo: © Ken Settle

THE NATURAL SIGN

Notice that a *natural sign* is used in the next tune to indicate a B-natural after a B-flat within the same measure. A natural sign returns a note that has been changed by an accidental to its unaltered position.

This bluesy tune uses ties to shift the emphasis off of the strong beats (beats 1 and 3) and onto the weak beats (beats 2 and 4). This is called *syncopation*.

Tied and True Blues

Try an organ sound with a strong, percussive attack.

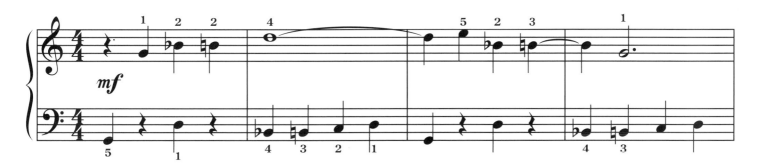

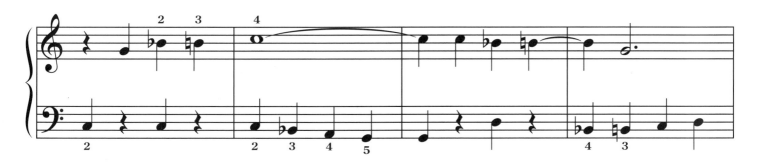

THE C MAJOR CHORD

A *chord* is a combination of three or more notes played together. The *root* of a chord is the note that gives the chord its name. The note C is the root of the *C major chord,* which is made up of the notes C–E–G.

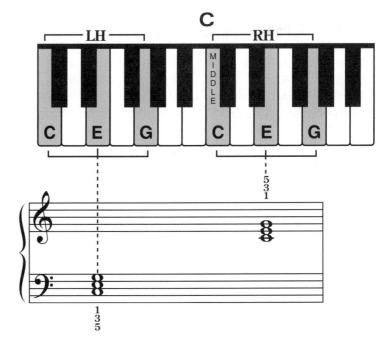

It is very important to play all three notes exactly together, keeping your fingers curved. Practice these C major chords with your left hand.

C Major Chord Warm-up (Left Hand)

Largo

(Theme from the New World Symphony)

> *Since this melody is from one of the most famous classical symphonies, try it with an orchestral string sound.*

Antonin Dvořák

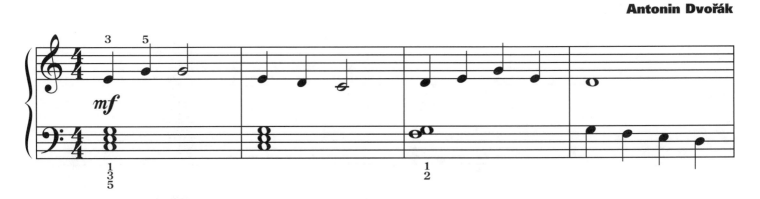

THE PICKUP

When one or more notes are played before the first full measure at the beginning of a piece, it is called a *pickup*. The pickup measure is an *incomplete measure*. Frequently, when a piece begins with a pickup, the last measure will also be incomplete so that the rhythmic values of the two combined equal one full measure.

Practice the C major chord with the right hand before playing "When the Saints Go Marching In."

C Major Chord Warm-up (Right Hand)

When the Saints Go Marching In

"When the Saints Go Marching In" is an American spiritual commonly played by New Orleans Dixieland jazz bands. It will sound great played with a brass sound.

American Spiritual

THE G⁷ CHORD

The G⁷ chord is frequently used with the C major chord. Notice that, unlike the C major chord, the root of this chord is not played as the lowest note. This is called an *inversion*.

G⁷

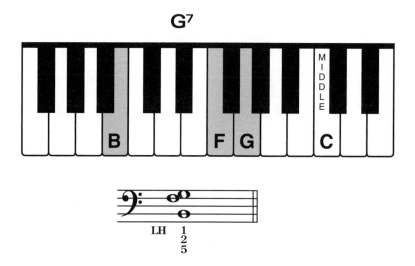

These exercises will help you learn to switch between playing the C and G⁷ chords.

No. 1

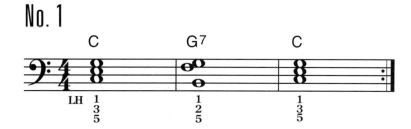

No. 2

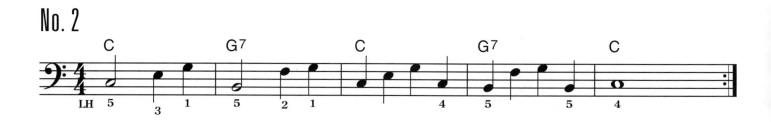

No. 3

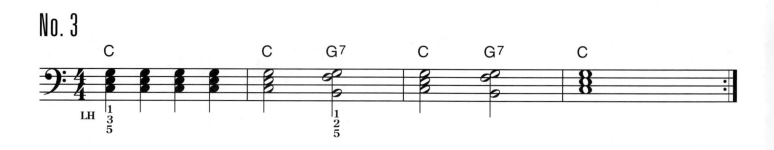

This piece has the melody in the right hand and combines harmonic
2nds and 3rds with chords in the left-hand accompaniment.

Mary Ann

Traditional

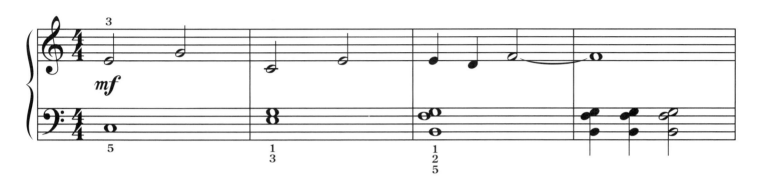

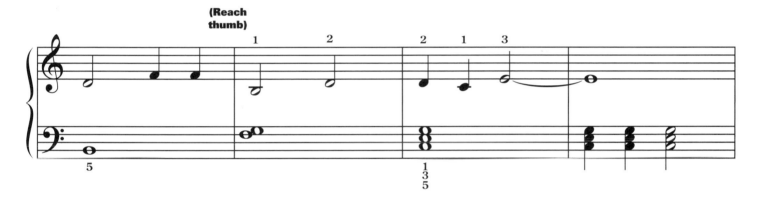

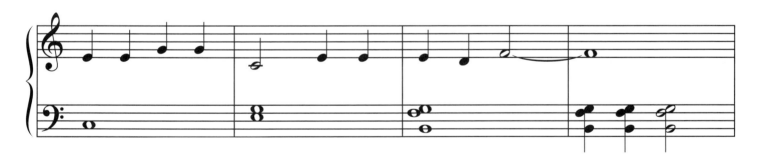

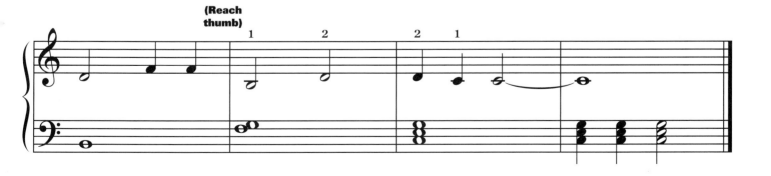

THE F MAJOR CHORD

The *F major chord* often appears with the C major and G7 chords. Like the G7 chord you learned on page 44, the F major chord you will play is an inversion.

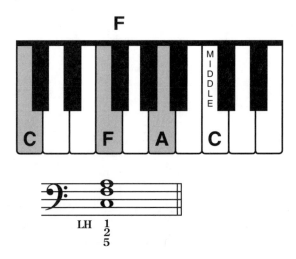

Practicing these exercises will help you learn to play the F major chord in combination with C major and G7.

No. 1

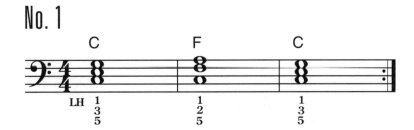

No. 2

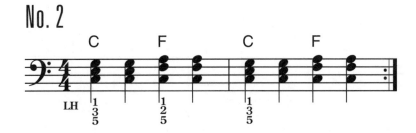

No. 3

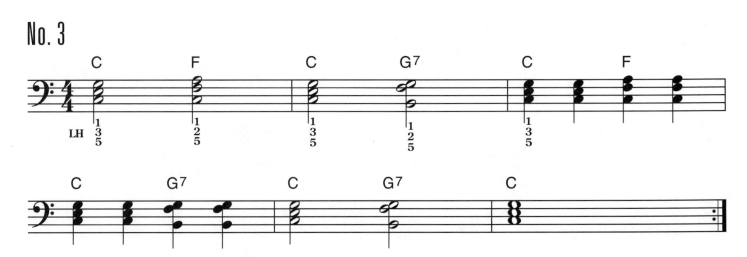

Congratulations! You've reached the end of Alfred's MAX™ Keyboard 1. You deserve a resounding rendition of this song to be sung in your honor. Change the name to "For She's a Jolly Good Lady" if necessary.

For He's a Jolly Good Fellow

Traditional English Folk Song

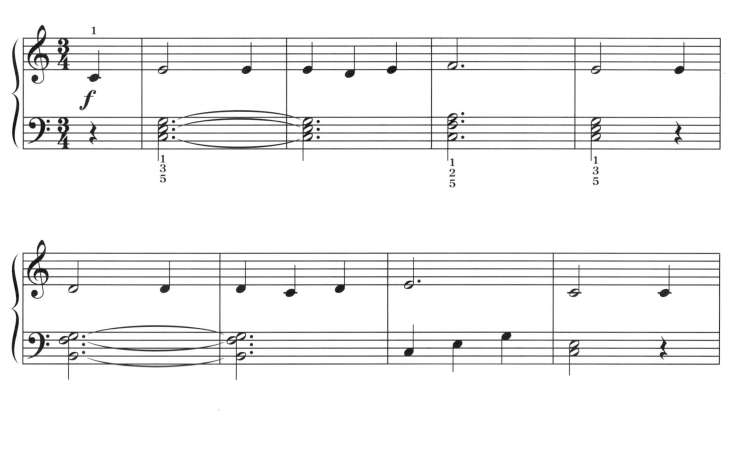

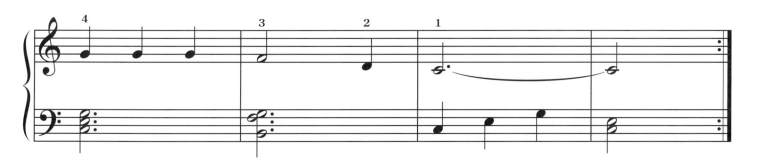

CERTIFICATE OF PROMOTION

This certifies that

_____

has mastered and perfected
Alfred's MAX™ Keyboard 1
and is hereby promoted to
Alfred's MAX™ Keyboard 2.

Teacher _____

Date _____